Going Up and Down

Story by Leonie Bennett
Pictures by Ian Cunliffe

Look at me!
I am going up.

I am going down.

I am going in.

I am going
in and out.
I am going out.

Look at me. I am going up and down.

Down!

I am going in...

...and out.

I am going round and round...

...and round and round.

Look at me. I am dizzy!